Cook Memorial Public Library

3 1122 01302 2079

DEC 1 0 2013

SO-AZQ-856

XTREME PETS
BUGS

BY S.L. HAMILTON

COOK MEMORIAL LIBRARY
413 N. MILWAUKEE AVE.
LIBERTYVILLE, ILLINOIS 60048

Visit us at
www.abdopublishing.com

Published by ABDO Publishing Company, PO Box 398166, Minneapolis, MN 55439.
Copyright ©2014 by Abdo Consulting Group, Inc. International copyrights reserved in all
countries. No part of this book may be reproduced in any form without written permission
from the publisher. A&D Xtreme™ is a trademark and logo of ABDO Publishing Company.

Printed in the United States of America, North Mankato, Minnesota.
032013
092013

Editor: John Hamilton
Graphic Design: Sue Hamilton
Cover Design: Sue Hamilton
Cover Photo: Thinkstock
Interior Photos: AP-pg 9 (budwing mantis), Corbis-pgs 4-5, 8 (ghost & Indian flower
mantises), 9 (dead leaf mantis), 12-13, 23 & 29; Getty-pgs 10, 11, 18-19, 20-21, & 24-25;
iStock-pg 28; Thinkstock-pgs 1, 2-3, 6-7, 8, 14-15, 16, 17, 22, 26-27, 30-31 & 32.

ABDO Booklinks
Web sites about Xtreme Pets are featured on our Book Links pages. These links are routinely
monitored and updated to provide the most current information available.
Web site: www.abdopublishing.com

Library of Congress Control Number: 2013931666

Cataloging-in-Publication Data

Hamilton, Sue
 Bugs / Sue Hamilton.
   p. cm. -- (Xtreme pets)
 ISBN 978-1-61783-970-2
 1. Insects--Juvenile literature. 2. Pets--Juvenile literature.   I. Title.
 595.7--dc23

                                                                    2013931666

CONTENTS

XTREME PETS: BUGS

There are more than 800,000 different types of insects. Bugs are very interesting pets. They are quiet, easy to care for, and fascinating to watch. Some are beautiful. Some are difficult to see because they are so well camouflaged. Some eat plants. Some eat other insects!

Katydid

XTREME FACT – More
than 75% of all animals
on Earth are insects.

PRAYING MANTISES

Named for the way they hold their limbs in a prayer-like position, praying mantises are one of the most popular bug pets. They live for about 10-14 months. Mantises often blend in with their surroundings, resembling green leaves, sticks, or flowers. They are meat eaters. Their spiky front legs snap out to grab and hold grasshoppers, crickets, moths, flies, and other insects.

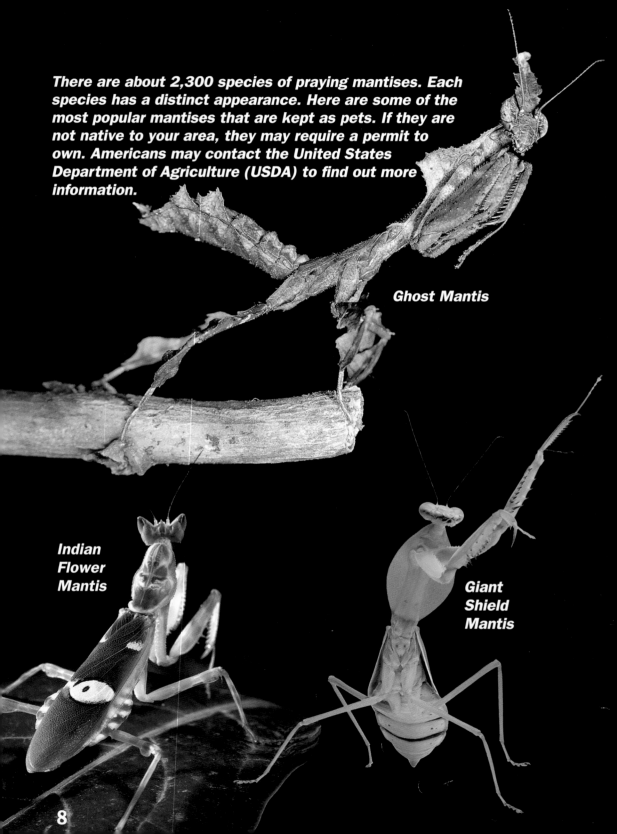

There are about 2,300 species of praying mantises. Each species has a distinct appearance. Here are some of the most popular mantises that are kept as pets. If they are not native to your area, they may require a permit to own. Americans may contact the United States Department of Agriculture (USDA) to find out more information.

Ghost Mantis

Indian Flower Mantis

Giant Shield Mantis

Budwing Mantis

Dead Leaf Mantis

Walking stick insects are part of a group called "phasmids." There are nearly 3,000 different species. They may live for 18-24 months. Unlike their carnivorous mantis cousins, these insects eat plants, such as romaine lettuce. They blend in with their surroundings. Their excellent camouflage makes them interesting pets to watch.

XTREME FACT – To defend themselves, walking sticks may pinch or bite. American walking sticks have a bad-smelling spray that has been known to cause temporary blindness.

Northern walking sticks are popular pets. They may live for six months to a year. Walking sticks molt, or shed their outer layer, as they grow. They reproduce easily, and a second generation may be born from the first.

Northern Walking Stick

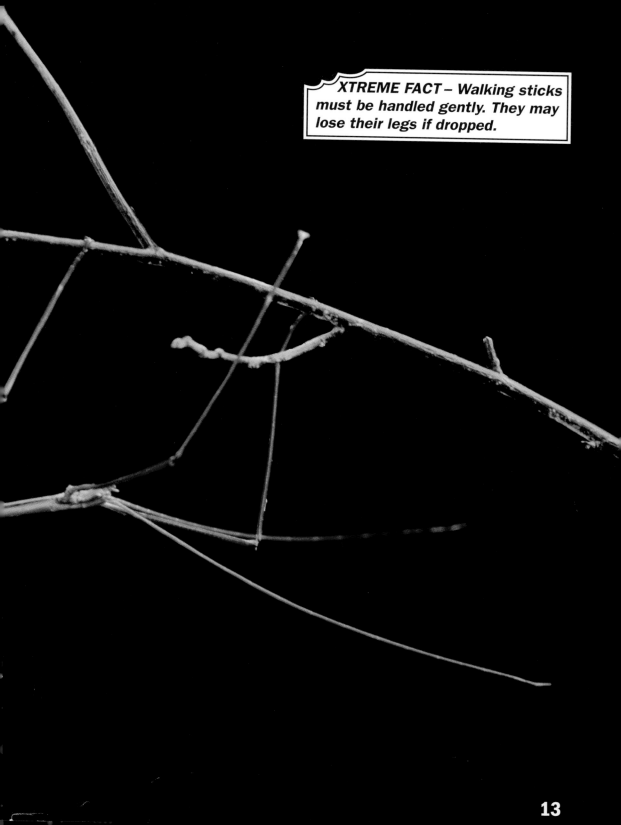

XTREME FACT – Walking sticks must be handled gently. They may lose their legs if dropped.

ANTS

Ants are busy workers and fun to watch. Many commercial "ant farms" are available that allow owners to see their ants create tunnels, eat, and store food. Ants require little care, although they must have a small amount of water and food, such as bread crumbs.

There are about 10,000 species of ants. Some popular ant pets are black ants, red ants, fire ants, and carpenter ants. Ants live for about one to three months.

XTREME FACT – The study and keeping of ants is called myrmecology.

BEETLES

Beetles are symbols of strength and good luck. Stag beetles, Hercules beetles, elephant beetles, and rhinoceros beetles are often kept as pets. While beetles may only live for six months, they are fascinating to watch grow from a worm-like larvae, or grub, into an adult. Beetles eat fruits and vegetables.

Larvae or Grub

Pupa

Adult Hercules Beetle (male)

Rhinoceros Beetles

Xtreme Fact – In Japan, a gambling game calls for two male rhinoceros beetles to be placed on a log. People bet on which beetle will knock the other off the log.

Male elephant beetles may grow to 5 inches (13 cm) in length!

Elephant Beetle

COCKROACHES

Some cockroaches are pests, but some make interesting pets. Madagascar hissing cockroaches "hiss" when they are alarmed and during mating. They may live for five years. Roaches eat fruit, vegetables, and dry pet food. They are good climbers and must be kept in a tank with a locked lid.

Madagascar Hissing Cockroach

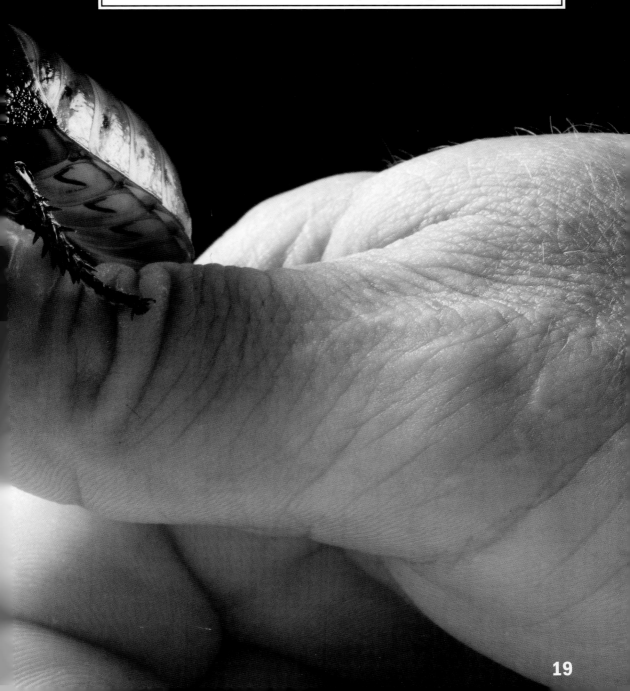

MILLIPEDES

Giant African millipedes and North American millipedes are popular, easy-going pets.

XTREME FACT – Millipede means "1,000 feet." While they do have many legs (two per body segment), they don't have 1,000.

Millipedes are born from eggs. They molt as they grow. These multi-legged myriapods may grow to be 12 inches (30 cm) long. Millipedes live from one to 10 years. They eat fruit and vegetables, as well as rotting wood and leaves. Owners enjoy finding their millipede's favorite food.

Giant African Millipede

GRASSHOPPERS

Grasshoppers are easy pets to care for. They may live up to a year in an aquarium or straw cage.

Grasshoppers eat grass and other plants. They are fragile creatures and must be handled gently. If frightened, a grasshopper may spit a non-dangerous brown liquid that some people call "tobacco juice." Grasshoppers are fun to watch grow and are known for catapulting themselves in giant leaps and bounds.

XTREME FACT – A full-grown grasshopper can jump as high as 10 times its own body length. It can leap 20 times its length horizontally. Grasshoppers also have wings and can fly.

CRICKETS

Crickets have been kept as pets for centuries. Some people consider them a sign of good luck. Male crickets "sing." They do this by rubbing their wing covers against each other. The singing is used to attract female crickets. Many people find the sound soothing.

Crickets live for about one or two months. They are good escape artists, so a container with a tight lid and air holes is necessary. They need some kind of hiding place, such as an empty egg carton. Crickets eat fruit and green vegetables and must have a small amount of fresh water.

XTREME FACT – A cricket "sings" faster or slower depending on the surrounding air temperature. A person can guess the temperature by counting a cricket's chirps over 14 seconds and then adding 40. For example: 35 Chirps + 40 = 75 degrees Fahrenheit (24°C).

KATYDIDS

Katydids are related to grasshoppers and crickets. They all belong to a group (order) called orthoptera, which means "straight wings."

Katydids are named for the call they make: "Katydid! Katydidn't!" They are usually found on plants during the hottest part of the day. Most katydids are green and resemble leaves, which is mainly what they eat. Katydids will live for a few weeks up to three months.

Katydid

XTREME FACT – A katydid's antennae may grow to be two-to-three times as long as its body. It uses its antennae for touch and smell, helping it find food and mates.

Luna Moths

The beautiful luna moth is one of the largest moth species. It has a wing span of 4 inches (10 cm). As pets, they are interesting to watch grow and change. Eggs hatch within 10-12 days of being laid. They emerge as caterpillars and immediately begin eating persimmon, walnut, or sycamore leaves. As they grow over the next four weeks, they shed their skins about five times. They then spin cocoons around themselves and lay dormant.

Luna Moth Caterpillar

XTREME FACT – Adult luna moths do not have mouths and are unable to eat.

In about three weeks luna moths emerge from their cocoons. During the day, they sit perfectly still. At night, luna moths are wildly busy, flying about and looking for mates. Adults live about a week, which is just long enough to reproduce.

GLOSSARY

CAMOUFLAGE
External coloring on an insect that allows it to blend in with its surroundings.

CARNIVOROUS
A creature that eats meat in order to survive.

DORMANT
Alive, but not moving. Insects such a moths and butterflies spin cocoons around themselves and lay dormant for a period of time as they change from caterpillars into their adult forms.

LARVAE
A newly hatched insect, usually worm-like in shape, that has yet to change into its adult form.

MOLT
Insects shed their outer layer, or molt, in order to grow bigger. Many insects molt several times before reaching adulthood. Some insects eat their molted outer layer.

MYRIAPODS

A class of insects that include creatures with multiple body segments, of which each segment has legs. Millipedes and centipedes are part of this group of insects.

OOTHECA

A cocoon-like case that holds the eggs of such insects as roaches and mantises.

ORTHOPTERA

A class of insects that includes grasshoppers, crickets, katydids, cockroaches, and mantises. These insects have mandibles, strong beak-like mouth organs that are used for grabbing and biting their food.

PHASMIDS

A class of long, thin insects, such as walking sticks, that feed on plants.

PUPA

The middle stage of some insects' lives, such as beetles, between larvae and adult. Bugs are inactive and nonfeeding at this stage.

SPECIES

A group of living things that have similar looks and behaviors, but are not identical. They are often called by a similar name. For example, there are about 10,000 species of ants.

INDEX